D0244939

**Frantic Assembly
and the National Theatre of Scotland present**

BEAUTIFUL BURNOUT

by Bryony Lavery

Beautiful Burnout was first performed
on Saturday 7 August 2010 at Pleasance Forth, Edinburgh.

Please note that this production contains strobe lighting, haze effects,
loud music and strong language.

The Scottish
Government

LOTTERY FUNDED

Supported using public funding by
**ARTS COUNCIL
ENGLAND**

Cast

in alphabetical order

Margaret Ann Bain	**Dina Massie**
Ali Craig	**Ainsley Binnie**
Keith Fleming	**Bobby Burgess**
Taqi Nazeer	**Ajay Chopra**
Julie Wilson Nimmo	**Carlotta Burns**
Stuart Ryan	**Cameron Burns**
Matthew Trevannion	**Steve George / Neil Neill**

Creative Team

Bryony Lavery	**Writer**
Underworld	**Music**
Laura Hopkins	**Designer**
Andy Purves	**Lighting Designer**
Carolyn Downing	**Sound Designer**
Ian William Galloway	**Video Designer**
Eddie Kay	**Associate Director (Movement)**
Neil Bettles	**Associate Director (Tour)**
Anne Henderson	**Casting Director**
Richard Ryder	**Dialect and Voice Coach**

Directed by Scott Graham and Steven Hoggett
Choreographed by the Directors with the original 2010 Company

Production Team

David Harraway	**Production Manager**
Nick Hill	**Company Stage Manager**
Sarah Thomas	**Deputy Stage Manager**
Sam Thornber	**Technical Stage Manager**
Douglas Green	**Lighting Supervisor**
Giles Thomas	**Sound and Video Supervisor**
Kat Smith	**Wardrobe Supervisor**
Tamsin Withers	**Production Assistant**

Thanks

Frantic Assembly and the National Theatre of Scotland wish to thank the following individuals and organisations for their support.

Theatre Royal Plymouth and all at TR2.

Boxing Consultation and Training
Brian Donald, Danny Lee (Greenock Amateur Boxing Club), Terry McCormack (Lochend Amateur Boxing Club), Bruce Silverglade (Gleason's Gym, Brooklyn), Kevin Smith and Dr Brian Tansey.

Previous *Beautiful Burnout* Companies
Joni Carter, Jon Clarence, Hilary Cross, Blythe Duff, Andrew Elliot, Ryan Fletcher, Rachel Godding, Kevin Guthrie, Nick Hill, Sunita Hinduja, Eddie Kay, Katy Lonsdale, Vicki Manderson, Stuart Martin, Lorraine M McIntosh, Henry Pettigrew, Neill Pollard, Kat Smith, Ewan Stewart and Adam Young.

Cast Biographies

Margaret Ann Bain
Dina Massie

Margaret trained at the Drama Studio London.

Her theatre credits include *Henry V* (Theatre Delicatessen/Latitude Festival), *A Doll's House* (Theatre Delicatessen/Latitude Festival), *3 Stories* (Rough Fiction/People at Play), *The Love of the Nightingale* (Rough Fiction), *It's A Girl* (The Weaver Hughes Ensemble/Wonderland Production), *Kid Simple: A Radio Play in the Flesh* (Open Plan Productions) and *After Columbus* (Pedlar Productions).

Film credits include *Zero Tolerance* (Tomcat Productions), *The Dead Are Silent* (Everything is Okay Ltd) and *Making Ugly* (Squarebox Yellow/Vernon Films).

Television credits include *Crisis Control* (BBC) and *Lady Randy – Churchill's Mother* (Flame TV/Channel 4).

Ali Craig
Ainsley Binnie

Ali trained at Mountview Academy of Performance Art.

His National Theatre of Scotland credits include *Macbeth* and *The Making of Us*. Ali was also a member of the original cast of the National Theatre of Scotland's multi-award-winning *Black Watch* and toured with the production in the UK and internationally between 2006 and 2008.

Other theatre credits include *Hamlet* (Greenwich), *Waterproof* (Òran Mór) and *The Rocky Horror Show* (European tour).

Film credits include *Pelican Blood, The Good Times are Killing Me* and *The Making of Us.*

Television credits include *Monarch of the Glen* and *Sea of Souls*.

Keith Fleming
Bobby Burgess

Keith trained at the Guildhall School of Music and Drama.

His National Theatre of Scotland credits include *The Making of Us, Black Watch, The Miracle Man* and *Peer Gynt*, for which he was awarded Best Male Performance at the 2007-08 Critics' Awards for Theatre in Scotland, and nominated for Best Actor at the 2008 TMA Awards.

Other theatre credits include *Stones in his Pockets* (Tron), *The Dark Things* (Traverse, Edinburgh), *Doubt, Autobahn, Days of Wine and Roses* (Theatre Jezebel), *Barflies* (Grid Iron), *Sunshine on Leith, Scenes from an Execution, Cabaret, Mince?, Twelfth Night, Macbeth, Rum and Vodka* and many more as a member of Dundee Rep Ensemble.

Film and television credits include *Kings of the Wild Frontier* and *Split Second*.

Taqi Nazeer
Ajay Chopra

Taqi studied at the Royal Conservatoire of Scotland.

His professional debut was with *Beautiful Burnout* at the Edinburgh Festival Fringe 2010. He has performed internationally with the show at St Ann's Warehouse (New York), Sydney Festival, Perth International Arts Festival and New Zealand International Arts Festival.

Short Film credits include *Lost* (Dir. Lee Paterson), *Homecoming* (GMAC/UK Film Council) and *Urban Anxieties: 3 Minute Wonder* (Channel 4).

Julie Wilson Nimmo
Carlotta Burns

Julie trained at the Royal Conservatoire of Scotland.

Her National Theatre of Scotland credits include Lily in *Men Should Weep* (National Tour), Agnes in *The House of Bernarda Alba, 365* (National Theatre of Scotland/Edinburgh International Festival/Lyric Hammersmith) and *Tutti Frutti*.

Other theatre credits include Leyla in *Double Nugget* (Random Accomplice), Mary in *Corstorphine Road Nativity* (Festival Theatre Edinburgh), *Aladdin* (First Family), *Balamory Live* (DC Entertainment), *Shining Souls* (Tron) and *The Magic Island* (TAG).

Television credits include Winnifred in *Blue Haven*, Elizabeth Macquarie in *Lachlan Macquarie: The Father of Australia, Pulp Video, Taggart, Big Bad World II, Balamory, Chewin' the Fat, Murder Rooms, Rab C Nesbitt, Stand and Deliver, The Baldy Man* and *The Young Person's Guide to Becoming a Rock Star*.

Film credits include *After Life, Mrs Caldicot's Cabbage War, My Life So Far, The Debt Collector, The Slab Boys* and *The Wrong Blonde*.

Radio credits include *Trials of Tommy, Cuba, Leach Hill* and *Fags, Mags and Bags*.

Stuart Ryan
Cameron Burns

Stuart is a recent graduate from Central School of Speech and Drama. *Beautiful Burnout* marks his professional debut.

Theatre roles while training include Sorin in *The Seagull*, Don Jon in *Much Ado About Nothing*, Richard Lorey in *To Be Taken with Water*, Servant in *School for Scandal*, Malcolm in *Macbeth*, Amstid in *As I Lay Dying*, Orestes in *Electra Garrigo* and Flaminio in *Banished*.

Film and television credits include *How Not to Live Your Life* (BBC3) and *Richard II* (BYFA).

Matthew Trevannion
Steve George / Neil Neill

Matthew's previous work for Frantic Assembly includes *Little Dogs* (with National Theatre Wales).

Other theatre credits include Ensemble in *Dr Dee* (English National Opera), Driscoll in *The Sea Plays* (Old Vic Tunnels), Ensemble in *Hamlet* (Young Vic), Mikey in *Love Steals Us From Loneliness* (National Theatre Wales), Paul in *Virtual Real* (Assembly Rooms/Roundhouse Theatre), Jake in *All in All* (Rosencratz Theatre), Jack in *Bright Unconquered Sons* (Pleasance Theatre), Kreon in *Antigone* (BAC), Lee Baum in *The American Clock* (BAC) and Stig in *Stig of the Dump* (Hereford Courtyard Theatre).

Alongside acting, Matthew's first play as a writer, *Bruised*, was produced by Theatre Clywd this summer. His next play, *Geared*, has been commissioned by National Theatre Wales.

Creative Team Biographies

Bryony Lavery
Writer

Bryony Lavery's plays include *Her Aching Heart* (Pink Paper Play of the Year 1992), *Last Easter* and *A Wedding Story* (2000). Her play *Frozen*, commissioned by Birmingham Rep, won the TMA Best Play Award, the Eileen Anderson Central Television Award, was produced on Broadway where it was nominated for four Tony awards. Her Frantic Assembly piece, *Stockholm* won the Wolff-Whiting award for Best Play of 2008.

Her recent work includes *Kursk* with Sound and Fury at The Young Vic UK and Sydney Opera House, *A Christmas Carol* at West Yorkshire Playhouse and an adaptation of *The £1,000,000 Bank Note* for BBC Radio 4.

Future plans include *Thursday* for ETT/Brink, *Cesario* for National Theatre, *Dirt* for Studio Theatre, Washington DC and an adaptation of Armistead Maupin's *Tales of The City* for Radio 4.

Bryony is honorary Doctor of Arts at De Montfort University and a Fellow of The Royal Society of Literature.

Scott Graham
Co-Director/ Choreographer

Scott Graham is co-founder and Artistic Director of Frantic Assembly. For Frantic, Scott has co-directed *Little Dogs* (with National Theatre Wales),

Lovesong, Beautiful Burnout (with National Theatre of Scotland, Fringe First),
Othello (TMA award – Best Direction), *Stockholm* (including a 2010 revival for
Sydney Theatre Company), *pool (no water), Dirty Wonderland, Rabbit,
Peepshow* and *Underworld.* Director/performer credits include *Hymns, Tiny
Dynamite, On Blindness, Heavenly, Sell Out, Zero, Flesh, Klub* and *Look Back In
Anger.* Scott Graham's other directing credits include: *Home* (National Theatre
of Scotland) *Ker-ching* (Sixth Sense), *It's A Long Road* and *Up on the Roof* (Polka
Theatre). Scott has also provided choreography and movement direction for *The
Curious Incident of the Dog in the Night-time* (National Theatre), *Dr Dee*
(Manchester International Festival/English National Opera), *Beauty and the
Beast* and *Cinderella* (Unicorn Theatre), *Frankenstein* (Royal and Derngate); *The
May Queen* (Liverpool Everyman), *Hothouse* and *Market Boy* (National Theatre),
Villette (Stephen Joseph Theatre), *Vs* (Karim Tonsi Dance Company, Cairo),
Improper (Bare Bones Dance Company), *Dazzling Medusa* and *A Bear Called
Paddington* (Polka) and *Stuart Little* (No 1 tour). With Steven Hoggett and
Bryony Lavery, Scott created *It Snows,* a National Theatre Connections play for
2008. With Steven Hoggett, Scott has written *The Frantic Assembly Book of
Devising Theatre* (Routledge).

Steven Hoggett
Co-Director/ Choreographer

Steven Hoggett is co-founder and Artistic Director of Frantic Assembly. For
Frantic Assembly, Steven has co-directed *Little Dogs* (with National Theatre
Wales), *Lovesong, Beautiful Burnout* (with National Theatre of Scotland, Fringe
First), *Othello* (TMA award – Best Direction), *Stockholm* (including a 2010 revival
for Sydney Theatre Company), *pool (no water), Dirty Wonderland, Rabbit,
Peepshow and Underworld.* Director/performer credits for the company include
Hymns, Tiny Dynamite, On Blindness, Heavenly, Sell Out, Zero, Flesh, Klub and
Look Back In Anger. As Associate Director/Movement, Steven worked on the
multi award-winning production *Black Watch* (National Theatre of Scotland) for
which he received the 2009 Olivier award for Best Theatre Choreography. On
Broadway Steven has recently choreographed the Green Day musical *American
Idiot, Peter & the Starcatcher* (Lucille Lortel Award – Outstanding
Choreographer) and *Once* (Lucille Lortel Award – Outstanding Choreographer).
Steven has also provided choreography and movement direction for *The Curious
Incident of the Dog in the Night-time* (National Theatre), *Dr Dee* (Manchester
International Festival/English National Opera), *Hunter 365* (National Theatre of
Scotland), *Frankenstein* (Royal and Derngate), *Dido Queen of Carthage, The
Hothouse* and *Market Boy* (National Theatre), *The Bacchae* (National Theatre of
Scotland), *The Wolves In The Wall* (National Theatre of Scotland and Improbable),
Villette (Stephen Joseph Theatre), *Jerusalem* (West Yorkshire Playhouse),
Mercury Fur and *The Straits* (Paines Plough). With Scott Graham and Bryony
Lavery, Steven created *It Snows,* a National Theatre Connections play for 2008.
With Scott Graham, Steven has written *The Frantic Assembly Book of Devising
Theatre* (Routledge).

Laura Hopkins

Designer

Laura trained in interior design and at the Motley Theatre Design course.

Previous work for Frantic Assembly includes *Othello* and *Stockholm*. Her National Theatre of Scotland credits include *Black Watch*, *Peter Pan* and *The House of Bernarda Alba*.

Current and recent work includes *Love and Information* by Caryl Churchill (Royal Court, costumes), *Soul Sister* (Hackney Empire/Savoy Theatre/Tour), *Troilus and Cressida* (Royal Shakespeare Company co-production with the Wooster Group), *Midsummer Night's Dream* and *Ragtime* (Regents Park Open Air Theatre).

Other work includes *You Can't Take It With You* (Royal Exchange, Manchester), *The Death of Klinghoffer* (English National Opera/Metropolitan Opera, New York), *Juliet and Her Romeo* (Bristol Old Vic), *Shoes* (Sadlers Wells and Peacock Theatre), *King Lear* (Chile, Dir. Pete Brooks), *A Delicate Balance* by Edward Albee (Almeida), *Lullaby* and *Gross Indecency* (Duckie), *Kellerman* and *Hotel Methuselah* (Imitating the Dog and Pete Brooks), *Time and the Conways* (National Theatre), *Rough Crossings* (Headlong), *Faustus* (TMA award winner - Best Design), *Hamlet, Othello* (Northampton, and then on tour with Headlong, also nominated for TMA award), with Dir. Tim Carroll *Merchant of Venice* (Royal Shakespeare Company), *Peer Gynt* (Guthrie Theatre, Minneapolis), *Golden Ass, Macbeth, Storm* (Globe Theatre) and *Adolf Hitler: My Part in His Downfall* (Spike Milligan, tour).

Previous work includes *Rudolf* (costumes, Vienna), The INS Broadcasting Unit at the ICA (collaboration with author Tom McCarthy), *Cosi fan tutte* and *Falstaff* (English National Opera), *Falstaff* (Opera North), *Sinatra* (costumes, London Palladium and tour), *Jerusalem* (West Yorkshire Playhouse, nominated for a TMA award), *Mister Heracles* (TMA award for Best Design), *Elixir of Love* (New Zealand Opera), *Carnesky's Ghost Train* (a visual theatre ride), *Swan Lake Re-mixed* (Volksoper, Vienna) and *The Rake's Progress* (Welsh National Opera).

Andy Purves

Lighting Designer

Andy is a lighting designer and creative technician working primarily in visual and movement-based theatre, circus and on projects in found space. Andy trained in sound and lighting engineering at the University of Derby and has an MA in lighting design and theatre-making from Central School of Speech and Drama, where he also tutors in lighting.

Previous work for Frantic Assembly includes *Little Dogs* (with National Theatre Wales), *Lovesong* and *Stockholm.*

Lighting design projects include *Mess* (Caroline Horton), *The Irish Giant* (Cartoon de Salvo), *The Arrival* (Tamasha/Circus Space), *Babel* (Stan Won't Dance), *The Erpingham Camp* (Hydrocracker/Brighton Festival), *Ida Barr*, *Office Party*

(Barbican), *Frankenstein* (Northampton Royal), *Home Inverness* (National Theatre of Scotland), *Outre* and *Ren-Sa* (Array).

He designs regularly for Circus Space, has toured extensively with Propeller, Frantic Assembly, The National Theatre of Scotland and Spymonkey, has worked for Brighton and Greenwich and Docklands Festivals and on *La Clique* and *La Soiree* at The Roundhouse and in the West End.

Carolyn Downing
Sound Designer

Previous work for Frantic Assembly includes *Little Dogs* (with National Theatre Wales) and *Lovesong.*

Sound design credits include *Double Feature* (National Theatre), *King John, The Gods Weep*, *The Winter's Tale, Pericles, Days of Significance* (Royal Shakespeare Company), *The Witness, Our Private Life*, *Oxford Street, Alaska* (Royal Court, JTU), *Amerika, Krieg der Bilder* (Staatstheater Mainz, Germany), *After Dido* (English National Opera at Young Vic), *Lower Ninth, Dimetos, Absurdia* (Donmar Warehouse), *All My Sons* (Schoenfeld Theatre, New York), *Tre Kroner - Gustav III* (Royal Dramatic Theatre, Sweden), *Angels in America: Millennium Approaches & Perestroika* (Headlong Theatre), *The Country Wife, A Whistle In The Dark, Moonshed* (Royal Exchange Theatre), *3rd Ring Out* (Metis Arts), *Gambling* (Soho Theatre), *Lulu, The Kreutzer Sonata, Vanya, State Of Emergency, The Internationalist* (Gate Theatre), *After Miss Julie, Ghosts, Dirty Butterfly* (Young Vic), *Belongings* (Hampstead), *After Miss Julie, Othello* (Salisbury Playhouse), *Moonlight & Magnolias* (Tricycle Theatre), *Andersen's English, Flight Path* (Out Of Joint), *Topdog/Underdog* (Sheffield Crucible Studio), *Is That All There Is, Hysteria* (Inspector Sands), *Arsenic and Old Lace* (Derby Playhouse), *The Water Engine* (Theatre 503, in association with The Young Vic), *Blood Wedding* (Almeida), *Gone To Earth* (Shared Experience), *No Way Out* (Huis Clos), *Stallerhof* (Southwark Playhouse) and *The Watery Part of the World* (Sound & Fury).

Ian William Galloway
Video Designer

Ian is a director, designer and filmmaker working with all forms of video for live performance.

Previous work for Frantic Assembly includes *Lovesong*. His National Theatre of Scotland credits include *Macbeth, Where the Wilds Things Are* and *The Missing*.

Theatre credits include *A Marvellous Year for Plums* (Chichester Festival Theatre), *The Pirate Project* (Improbable), *The Lion in Winter* (Theatre Royal Haymarket), *Singin' in The Rain* (Chichester Festival Theatre and West End), *Flashdance* (West End), *The Tempest* (Theatre Royal Haymarket), *A Midsummer Night's Dream* (Headlong), *The Kreutzer Sonata, Medea/ Medea, Nocturnal* (Gate Theatre), *The Gods Weep* (Royal Shakespeare Company), *Freerun*

(Udderbelly), *Midnight Your Time* (Hightide), *Hitchcock Blonde* (Alley Theatre, Houston & South Coast Repertory, LA), *A Minute Too Late* (Complicite), *EPIC* (Foster & Dechery), *Proper Clever* (Liverpool Playhouse), *The Spanish Tragedy, On The Record* (Arcola) and *Bunny* (Nabokov Theatre).

Opera credits include *Sancta Susannah, Von Heute Auf Morgen* (Lyon Opera House), *Babur, The Lion's Face, Seven Angels* (The Opera Group), *Hotel de Pekin* (Nationale Reisopera) and *Les Enfants Terribles* (Arcola).

Ian has toured the UK, Europe and Japan as a musician, designed and directed projections for concerts (Leona Lewis, Tom Vek and Riz MC) and has directed music videos and shorts.

He works as part of Mesmer, a collective of video and projection designers working across theatre, dance, music, fashion and the arts.

Underworld

Underworld is Rick Smith and Karl Hyde - artists, composers, musicians and creative partners of over 30 years standing. Since taking inspiration in the early '90s from the UK's nascent club scene, Smith and Hyde have made experimental and electronic records that bend the accepted formula of dancefloor music.

Underworld's first album, *Dubnobasswithmyheadman*, was described by *Melody Maker* at the time as "the most important album since *The Stone Roses* and the best since *Screamadelica*." In the ensuing years, the band has successfully balanced critical and commercial success, releasing a string of heavily eulogised albums (*Second Toughest In The Infants*, *Beaucoup Fish*, *A Hundred Days Off*, *Oblivion With Bells* and *Barking*) whilst cementing a reputation as one of the most visceral and inspiring live bands on the planet.

As well as working together as Underworld, Smith and Hyde are founding partners in the design company Tomato.

After working with Danny Boyle on his adaptation of *Trainspotting,* the sci-fi thriller *Sunshine* and the 2011 stage production of *Frankenstein* at the National Theatre (for which they were nominated for an Olivier Award for Best Sound Design), Underworld were appointed musical directors for the opening ceremony of the London 2012 Olympic Games.

www.underworldlive.com

franticassembly

'The vibrant and visceral Frantic Assembly' *Independent*

Frantic Assembly creates thrilling, energetic and unforgettable theatre. The company attracts new and young audiences with work that reflects contemporary culture. Vivid and dynamic, Frantic Assembly's unique physical style combines movement, design, music and text.

Scott Graham and Steven Hoggett formed Frantic Assembly in 1994 (with producer Vicki Middleton). Scott and Steven have since performed in or directed all of the company's work. They seek to collaborate on original ideas with today's most exciting artists. Frantic Assembly has toured widely throughout the UK, building its reputation as one of the country's most exciting companies. Internationally Frantic Assembly has performed, created and collaborated in 30 different countries.

In addition to its productions Frantic Assembly operates an extensive Learn & Train programme introducing 6,000 participants a year to the company's process of creating theatre, in a wide variety of settings. Frantic Assembly also delivers Ignition, an innovative vocational training project for young men, particularly targeting those with little previous experience of the arts.

Productions

Little Dogs	Devised by the Company *In partnership with National Theatre Wales*	2012
Lovesong	Abi Morgan	2011
Beautiful Burnout	Bryony Lavery *In co-production with the National Theatre of Scotland*	2010
Stockholm	Bryony Lavery *Australian production with Sydney Theatre Company*	2010
Othello	William Shakespeare	2008
Stockholm	Bryony Lavery	2007
pool (no water)	Mark Ravenhill	2006
Dirty Wonderland	Michael Wynne	2005
On Blindness	Glyn Cannon	2004
Rabbit	Brendan Cowell	2003
Peepshow	Isabel Wright	2002
Heavenly	Scott Graham, Steven Hogget and Liam Steel	2002
Tiny Dynamite	Abi Morgan	2001
Underworld	Nicola McCartney	2000
Hymns	Chris O'Connel	1999
Sell Out	Michael Wynne	1998
Zero	Devised by the Company	1997
Flesh	Spencer Hazel	1996
Klub	Spencer Hazel	1995
Look Back in Anger	John Osborne	1994

Frantic Assembly is a charity registered in England and Wales 1113716

Follow us on Twitter **@franticassembly**

Visit our online forum **www.franticassembly.co.uk/forum**

To find out how you can support the work of Frantic Assembly visit
www.franticassembly.co.uk/support

[NATIONAL THEATRE OF SCOTLAND]

It is our ambition to make incredible theatre experiences for you, which will stay in your heart and mind long after you have gone home.

We tirelessly seek the stories which need to be told and retold, the voices which need to be heard and the sparks that need to be ignited. We do this with an ever-evolving community of play-makers, maverick thinkers and theatre crusaders. We try to be technically adventurous and fearlessly collaborative. We are what our artists, performers and participants make us. And with no building of our own, we have the freedom to go where our audiences and stories take us. There is no limit to what we believe theatre can be, no limit to the stories we are able to tell, no limit to the possibilities of our imaginations.

All of Scotland is our stage, and from here we perform to the world. We are a theatre of the imagination: a Theatre Without Walls.

National Theatre of Scotland
Civic House
26 Civic Street
Glasgow G4 9RH
T: +44 (0) 141 221 0970
F: +44 (0) 141 331 0589
E: info@nationaltheatrescotland.com

For the latest information on all our activities, visit our online home at
nationaltheatrescotland.com

Follow us on Twitter: **@NTSonline**
Find us on Facebook: **NationalTheatreScotland**

The National Theatre of Scotland is core funded by the Scottish Government.
The National Theatre of Scotland, a company limited by guarantee and registered in Scotland (SC234270), is a registered Scottish charity (SCO33377).

The Scottish Government

Year of Creative Scotland 2012

Beautiful Burnout 2012

Theatre Royal, Plymouth
3 – 6 October
www.theatreroyal.com

Warwick Arts Centre, Coventry
9 – 13 October
www.warwickartscentre.co.uk

artsdepot, London
16 – 19 October
 www.artsdepot.co.uk

Sherman Cymru, Cardiff
23 – 27 October
www.shermancymru.co.uk

Dundee Rep Theatre, Dundee
31 October – 3 November
www.dundeerep.co.uk

West Yorkshire Playhouse, Leeds
6 – 10 November
www.wyp.org.uk

Northern Stage, Newcastle
13 – 17 November
www.northernstage.co.uk

Nuffield Theatre, Southampton
20 – 24 November
www.nuffieldtheatre.co.uk

Hull Truck Theatre, Hull
27 November – 1 December
www.hulltruck.co.uk

Extensive Learn Resources are available for this production.
For further information about the online resource pack, videos
workshops and more visit **www.franticassembly.co.uk**

Production images on pages overleaf feature previous cast members.
Photos by Brett Boardman, Gavin Evans and Richard Termine.

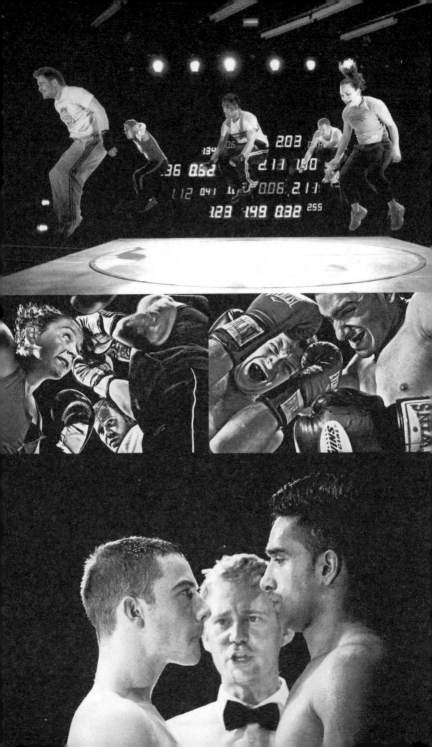

"be comfortable, be subtle, don't
chase the air. Dont try to
hurt fresh air..."
Kevin...

Refs only words:
Box.
Rope.
Break.

Track Listing

B.B v. 8   July '10

Morning   please help me
Food Chain
Ref #1   Hungerford Bridge
Gym Enter
2 Hours   No More
Fighting Fist   Ancient Phat Farm
Wren #1   Glem Bucket
Clobus / Scribble / Star   Scribble / ?? ♡'d Film??
Zanussi   Showlder
Dina School
SP24
Cheese Fridge
Amateur
Bobby's Eyes
Kitten! / Catch Up Pads   Kitten! / Bird
Promotion   ↓
Fridge Head
Get Yer Kit   ??
River
Handcream
Dina Space   River of Bass
2 Ajays   Monkey 2
Breath
Arrested / £   Dub Shepherd
Menace   Simple Peal
Wraps #2 / Refs / Spearmint   Geeza
Fight   Beautiful Burnout
Beautiful Burnout   ??
Ref #2   Slam!
One Punch   Crim!
Black Light2   To Heal

     ⟨post ... Diamond jigsaw? Coupon?⟩   FINN'S
                                           Food A Ready
                                           Boy!
                                           Geeza (ending)

Artistic Directors' Note

The idea for *Beautiful Burnout* initially came from a ten minute visit to Gleason's Gym, a world famous boxing gym in Brooklyn. It's quite hidden, just a doorway on a street. It was about 10 o'clock at night and the sweat, the focus, the smell, the energy, the noise, the intense application was mesmerising. It was one of those moments where you find yourself entering into a world that somehow you knew was there but never had any direct experience of.

We started talking about how to capture this experience within a show, how boxing shows we had seen had never quite presented a credible physicality. We felt inspired by the challenge of giving an audience that same visceral, thrilling and conflicting experience of the visit to Gleason's.

Watching boxing can come with its own moral dilemma. Boxing is often referred to as the "noble art", the "sweet science" by its supporters. It can be idolised and revered by academics and artists but even the people who love and appreciate it can often struggle to defend it morally. The willful infliction of damage upon an opponent is utterly abhorrent to others and has been considered a blood sport. There is a massive range of responses and reaction here. There's an incredible tension between those two points of view. That tension became really interesting for us to start grappling with.

Boxing is a provocative subject. We had no intention of shying away from the moral debate surrounding boxing. It is this debate that convinced us we had something to say about this world. The issue of how damage is both present and buried within a sport that appears to offer its participant's support, focus, and discipline is fascinating to both of us.

This show has toured across the UK, to New York, Sydney, Perth and Wellington. Everywhere we have gone we have met extraordinary people from the world of boxing. People who dedicate themselves to instilling others with a respect and commitment, which may otherwise have been missing from their lives. Yes, boxing can be brutal and cruel but it is also one of the most caring and inclusive families you could meet. These boxers and trainers have taught us so much, and their intensity and application remains an inspiration to us. Boxing is a world that is difficult to capture theatrically without falling into cliché but it is Bryony Lavery's and our intention to represent this world with honesty and integrity. We owe at least that to the people who gave their time, advice and guidance in making this show.

We would also like to recognise the tremendous input and encouragement of Neil Murray, Chris Hay and Jess Richards from the National Theatre of Scotland. And, as ever, thanks to Vicky Featherstone and John Tiffany for their wisdom and clarity.

We are incredibly excited about taking this show to new venues and new audiences again. As a touring company our commitment and passion is sharing invigorating work around the world. This interaction feeds our work. We hope you enjoy.

Bryony Lavery

Beautiful Burnout

faber and faber

First published in 2010
by Faber and Faber Limited
74–77 Great Russell Street
London WC1B 3DA

Reprinted with revisions to programme pages 2011
Reprinted with revisions to text 2012

Typeset by Country Setting, Kingsdown, Kent CT14 8ES
Printed and bound by CPI Group (UK) Ltd, Croydon, CR0 4YY

A CIP record for this book is available from the British Library

ISBN 978-0-571-30020-4

FSC
www.fsc.org
MIX
Paper from
responsible sources
FSC® C101712

2 4 6 8 10 9 7 5 3 1

Characters

in alphabetical order

Ainsley Binnie
a boxer

Bobby Burgess
a boxing trainer

Cameron Burns
a boxer

Carlotta Burns
a boxer's mother

Ajay Chopra
a boxer

Steve George
a referee

Dina Massie
a boxing lassie

Neil Neill
a boxer

The odd line lengths
weird   spacing
and plethora of exclamation marks
and question marks in the text
are the author's attempt to convey
the frenetic nature of these characters
in their situation!!!

/ in the text indicates one character
talking over another

SOME DICTIONARY DEFINITIONS

Time, *noun.* A limited stretch or space of continued existence, as the interval between two successive events or acts, or the period through which an action, condition, or state continues . . .

Beautiful, *adjective.* Very pleasing and impressive to listen to, touch, or especially to look at; very good or enjoyable.

Burnout, *noun.* Psychological exhaustion and diminished efficiency resulting from overwork or prolonged exposure to stress; somebody affected by psychological exhaustion. [*Informal.*] Failure of a machine or part of a machine to work because of overuse and excessive heat or friction; failure of a rocket or jet engine to work because the fuel supply has been exhausted or cut off.

BEAUTIFUL BURNOUT

We are always in and around a boxing ring.

Life is what happens in the few moments in,
during, around the obsessive path towards
becoming the brightest star in the night sky . . .

We are in a world of freely shared opinions
and self-promotion . . .

ONE
A REFEREE PREPARES

A square, raised boxing arena somewhere.

A referee, Steve George, watches footage of a boxing match . . .

Steve
He's refereeing impeccably . . .
Steve George
This seasoned professional . . .
This much-respected referee . . .
His job
Is to
Watch *like an eagle*
And 'protect the boxer without fear or favour' . . .
And this Steve George is a
Fucking beady-eyed fucking *golden* eagle!
He calls it.
There's a Winner
There's a Loser
But at the end of the day
Everyone's safe in the hands of this man.
Let's see that *again*, Boxing Aficionados!

(*Exits as . . .*
A washing machine rises out of the floor and . . .)

TWO
FOOD RUNS IN OUR FAMILY

Carlotta, a boxer's mum, arrives . . .

Carlotta

Welcome to the glamour of boxing!

Who *is* that Mysterious Figure loading the Zanussi??
Human Beings call me Carlotta ...
But ...
Under the *umbrella* title of *Mother*
I'm
Headcookcleanerbottlewasher*launderette*alarmclock
Small investment-vulnerable-lending-bank-with-over-
generous-overdraft-facilities ...
Bulk combiner of proteincarbsroughage

Calorie supplier

I feed The Beast.

Food runs in our family.
My gran was head dinner lady up at St Paul's
My dad worked at Tunnock's
My ex-husband *ate* food
My son *eats* food
I *cook* it
See how *that* works?

The only time my son doesnae eat *my* food
Is when he's on his two-week junkfood binge after a
fight ...
FishandchipsKFCMcdonaldsdeepfriedMarsbars
Oh Yes
All doon that mighty gullet into that ceaseless digestive
system
He has a taste for rubbish which he inherited from his
father

who now eats at another address

courtesy of a *Skank* name of Sheila Diver !
Skank!

Skank Shagger! . . .

Move *on*
Closure.

Otherwise . . .

(*Cameron, her son, climbs out of the washing
machine and takes off his sweaty gear for her laundry
attention.*)

At *this* eatery it's
Mince and tatties Monday
Steak pie Tuesday
Liver and bacon Wednesday
Thursday beef stew with carrots and onions oh *yes*!
Spaghetti bolognese I'm multi-cultural Friday
Saturday he's oot
Sunday roast dinner who makes the best roast
potatoes in *the world*

(*Cameron points to Carlotta.*)

I make the best roast potatoes in the world!!
Breakfast today is
Four boiled eggs toast and jelly beans . . .
Jelly beans!!
Eggs boiled for *three* minutes no more

Cameron
Like three minutes in boxing, Mum, nae mare nae less.

Carlotta
The *Future Champion* likes his eggs

Together
'Jest soft enough tae dip ma soldiers in!'

Carlotta
Three minutes 'nae mare nae less' it is.

(*Sings.*)

'Tii–i–ime
is on ma side
yes it es . . .'

(*Cameron exits.*)

My son sees me as quite *far* doon the food chain . . .
It goes
Famous Boxers Alive Or Dead
Any Boxers
Anybody who isnae a boxer but still knows anything
about boxing
Males
Fit Lassies
Lassies
Dogs
Cartoon Characters
Me.

No kidding   *jelly beans* for breakfast!
'Jelly beans is for energy'
Is that insane? Aye
Is ma son insane? Aye
Am I insane??
Hold that thought!

(*Carlotta exits as . . .*)

THREE
A SPLIT SECOND

Bobby Burgess enters, with water bottles, training bag.

Bobby
You pretend
It's fifteen minutes half an hour one investigative
session tops

Before
You know whether a boy's a boxer or not . . .
You watch them
Give them instructions
See if they listen
See if they can learn.

(*He sets out the bottles for training.*)

You say
'I'll watch you
See your style, I'll know in fifteen minutes
But
You're lying
Actually
It takes aboot five seconds . . .

No
Lying again
You know in a second

A *split* second
You've struck gold
Hit pay dirt
Found that rich seam
Dug up a *born* boxer   Eureka

He's called Ajay Chopra
He's a wee brun lad from Paisley
Already
He's subtle he's quick
He doesnae try to hurt fresh air . . .
He's the best lad at thes stage I've ever seen . . .

But   you keep *that* to *yourself*
Because . . .
Finding one's the easy part
Making one fulfil his promise?
Another story *altaegether*! . . .

They're all bloody silly testosteroned *teenagers*
Daft wee skelfs who think they know *everything* . . .
The section of society that knows the *least*
But believes they know *everything*
And therefore have minds *programmed* to *kibosh*
Any chance of personal success . . .

What do you do?
Try make them listen to *Reason*???
Wake Up!

Expect *Sense*???

Dream on!

You fucking *frighten* them

Boo!!!

Reign of Terror

Do as I say!

(*Everything does as he says.*)

Who rules the world? I rule the world!

(*All the world does as he says.*)

FOUR
TWO HOURS TWICE A WEEK

We're in the full glory of the gym . . .
    Young boxers Ajay Chopra, Ainsley Binney, Neil Neill,
Dina Massie appear from off, leap on to the square as . . .

Bobby
    Let's go, boys, let's go let's see you kill it

    It's your *shoulder* carries your guard

    Raise your guard

Raise your guard
Open your body
And close it

Remember . . .
Your jaw's connected to your legs!

Stay outside the distance
Stay outside the distance
Watch your man
Watch your *man*!!!

You're under *constant surveillance.*

It's *two* hours
Twice a week
In these two hours
Ye work as *hard* as ye can
As *much* as ye can!

All

Yes, Mr Burgess!

Bobby

No talking keep your breath for *boxing*!

Keep your balance at all times
Walking
Nice and relaxed nice and relaxed

Let your bones carry you

Slip to the inside
Slip to the outside

Step inside

Good

(*Cameron enters.*)

It's your ability to make people *miss*
Think all your wee moves, guys

Think your combinations, boys
Don't hold back you're only cheating yourself

(*To Cameron*.) In a minute, son . . .

Bobby

Be *comfortable*   be *subtle*
Don't chase the air
Don't try to hurt fresh air
That's no who you're trying to beat
Good
One minute!
Alright lads . . . take your wee sips . . .
You too, lassie . . .
Dinnae get dehydrated . . .
See my eyes
Wherever *you* are, *they* are
And I never sleep
They never close
I'm *watching* you
I'm seeing you
I'm prowling
I'm beading you
I have you in a *crossbeam* of concentration
Oh aye
Wee sips!
Your *rests* are important
Keep your minds switched *on*
I *know* when you switch off in there
These eyes can see into your brains . . .

(*To Cameron*.) Can I help you?

Cameron

I want to be one of these
The best one.

Bobby
Everyone wants to be 'the best one'
Right, lads?

Ajay / Neil / Ainsley / Dina
Right, Mr Burgess!

Bobby
And lassie.
This is our *Million Dollar Baby* . . .
Say 'Hello' to . . . ?

Cameron
Cameron   Burns

Ajay / Neil / Ainsley
Alright?

Cameron
Alright.
You train lassies?

Bobby
We train *this* one.
You got a problem with that?

Cameron
No   no problem

Dina
'No   no problem.' Wanker.

Bobby
Alright
Alright
Your minute's *up*
Good timekeeping's *essential*.

Water bottles *doon*
Okay, son

Eyes on me
Eyes *always* on me
That's the way to *catch up* with these other numpties.

(*And all eyes on Bobby as . . .*)

FIVE

A FIGHTING FIST LANDS
A HUNDRED PUNCHES IN THREE MINUTES

Bobby
It's *simple*.
A fighting fist lands a hundred punches per three-
minute round
You want to land as many punches
Per round as you can
Good punches means *points*
Calzaghe averaged nine-fifty tae a thousand per *match*
And that's what wears your opponent doon
It's what *wins*
You want to do it *right*!
Your hand's *delicate*
It contains twenty-seven bones
Striking a blow incorrectly can cause serious / damage
Develop a safe and solid punching fist

Ainsley
Carpals   *meta* carpals Right? Mr Burgess . . .

Ajay
Shut up

Neil Neill
I've only got two bones in / mine . . .

Ajay
Shut the fuck *up* . . .

Bobby

Excuse me???

Ajay / Neil / Ainsley

Sorry, Mr Burgess.

Bobby

Curl your fingers

(And they all . . .)

Tuck the tips in the middle of your palm
Fold your thumb over your fingers
It doesnae stick out beyond the line of your knuckles
Your fist should be lightly clenched
Until
Impact.

(They all . . .)

Punch in a straight line
It travels in a straight line
From the shoulder
The fist turns
Inward before impact
So only the flat knuckle part hits the target
This locks oot the arm
Ajay, show him

(And Ajay shows him . . .)

Ajay

The fist turns
Inward before impact
So only the flat knuckle part hits the target
This locks oot the arm
And rounds the shoulder
To protect the chin . . .

Bobby

Well remembered that, Chopra
Good.

Ajay

Four types of attack
The hook
The jab

Bobby

Southpaw

Ajay

Straight punch
To the head
To the body
Uppercut

To the body
To the chin

Bobby

Your target area is any point on the front or sides of
the head or body
Above the belt
And keep it *simple*
None ae that showboating shite!

Go on, son, show your style.

(*Cameron puts together some good punches.*)

Good
You know in a second
Born boxer.

Ajay

Born boxer, Bobby
No as pretty a colour as *me* though . . .

Bobby

No *cheek*, you.
There'll be no *colour* prejudice in *my* gym
Nothing wrong with bright *pink* . . .

Okay
I've had enough of your splendour for noo
Get oot of my hair.

Neil Neill

What hair, Mr Burgess?

Going, Mr Burgess.

Bobby

No you.
You stay.

(*Others exeunt, Cameron remains.*)

SIX
WELCOME TO MY STRANGE PLANET

Bobby shows Cameron how to wrap his hands as . . .

Bobby

This is *your* planet noo, Cameron Burns.
This is where *your* species survive.
Your DNA thrives in this rarefied atmosphere.

Cameron

Alright.

Bobby

This here's the last free gift you'll get from me
These are your wraps.

Either yourself
Or somebody stupid enough to care about you
. . . needs to get you
gloves bandages vests shorts warmup warndoon gear
boots   ask *Ajay*   the *brown* laddie   what's best to get
head guard a good one tae protect what brains you've
got in your head . . .

Cameron

Teachers say I've nae brains in there anyway . . .

Bobby

Do they?

Well . . . lucky for *you* . . .
I'll be your brains for you!
every Tuesday and Friday
Six p.m.
Sharp
Two hours twice a week nae latecomers
Nae fly-by-night I don't feel like it tonight I want tae watch
Feckin *Strictly-Come-EastEnders*!!!

Cameron

Aye   alright

Bobby

Ye need to look after these
They're your precision instruments.
This is a piece of Good Luck
That I'm handing you
We don't get given a big bag full of luck
People like us
An infinitesimally small few of us
Get
One little piece
Don't expect any more
Grab it
Grab your *one* piece of luck
This is your chance, Cameron Burns.

Make your parents proud of you
Much more important . . .
Make me proud of you

Cameron

Ontae it!

Bobby

Put em *up*!
Up.

(*And he's in stance.*)

SEVEN

EVEN THE CLOSEST STAR TAKES
FOUR YEARS FOR ITS LIGHT TO REACH US

Bobby

Good
Okay
Let's get doon tae business!
See *this*?

(*Three-minute clocks . . .*)

That's *your* face now.
That's the machinery what's ticking inside your brain
You're all Human Clocks
From now on, you'll be living your life in three-minute
bursts
From now on, you're no made up of flesh and bone . . .
You're made of *minutes*
Your minutes are made ae *seconds*
In which you need tae move and think faster than the
speed of light.
Seconds full of *activity* and   *choices*

You need tae keep your clock *ticking* so
Let's set you in perpetual motion

(*Other young boxers enter as . . .*)

Burpies
Here
Press-ups
Here
Sit-ups
Here
Star jumps   *full* stretch
Here
Three Minutes of your valuable time on each one
Full commitment
Clocks
Start ticking
Go!

(*And an intensive workout then . . .*
    Cameron at home.)

Carlotta
You get pregnant
You get married
So he'll get his father's name . . .

Cameron (*contempt*)
Burns!

Carlotta
You give him
Life
Breath
You give him, because of your famously generous
spirit
Your favourite name for a boy . . .

Cameron
Cameron!
Cameron Burns!

Carlotta
What's wrong with Cameron Burns?
It's a *lovely* name.

Cameron
It's a *shite* name!
A boxer needs something that says 'Legend'
James 'Bonecrusher' Smith!
Hector 'Macho' Camacho . . .
'Iron' Mike Tyson
Something that *captures* attention
Something that stands oot!

Carlotta
Okay . . .
How about Cameron 'Serious' Burns?

Cameron
Oh   *funny.*

Carlotta
How about
Cameron 'Third-Degree' Burns?!?!

Cameron
Hi   lar   i   ous
I'll go ask my dad . . .

Carlotta
Okay.
What are the other little 'bonecrushers' called?

(*And, as Cameron names them, they are there, in their
secret dreams . . .*)

Cameron
There's Neil Neill, Fists of Steel

Carlotta
Neil *Neill* . . .
Imaginative parents . . .

Cameron
Neil Neill 'so-good-they-named him *twice*' Fists of
Steel!

Carlotta

Well, pardon me!

Cameron

Ajay . . . 'The Dangerous *Cobra*' . . .

Carlotta

You could be Cameron 'The Idle *Pig*'!

Cameron

. . . 'The *Amazing* Ainsley Binnie'

Carlotta

'The *Untidy* Cameron Burns!'
Why is Ainsley Binnie *amazing*?

Cameron

He *knows* shite.
He *googles* shite.
He *says* shite,
And the *girl* . . . is
'Dina Massie the Battling Lassie . . .'
But *we* call her *Tits o' Terror*

(*Which is high wit . . .*)

Carlotta

Well . . . you could be
'*Brains of Fudge*'
'*Farts of / Fury*'

Cameron

Okay, I'm going round Dad and Sheila's . . .

Carlotta

Okay . . .
'*Fists* of Fury'
. . .?

Cameron

Fists of . . .
That might work . . .

Carlotta

Please!
No praise!
Now
'Cameron Burns – Fists of Fury . . .'
Move like a butterfly sting like a bee outta my way!

(*And she exits as Cameron goes towards the other names in boxing.*)

Ainsley

Did you know, Dina . . .
Astronomy-wise . . .
Even the closest star takes four years for the *light alone* to reach us
And is a massive, luminous ball of plasma held together by gravity?
Fact.

Neil Neill

I know *you're* a massive luminous ball of *shite* held together by gravity
Fact

Dina

Shut it, Fists ae Fuck
You!

Ainsley

Yes, Dina . . .

Dina

Just for future reference, *Binnie*!
This   is how much space I require around me!!!
This is where you don't step beyond!
Now
Out of My Space You Fucking Fanny!

(*Cameron Burns, Fists of Fury, bounces in.*)

Cameron
Here he is
The future star!

Neil Neill
Star, are you?

(*They surround him.*)

Why's that then?

(*They each take a hand or foot, pin him down, make him star-shaped.*)

Oh, aye, *star-shaped alright*!
Don't mess with 'Neil Neill Fists of Steel'.

(*Cameron is a pinned wriggling starfish.*)

Cameron
Don't mess with 'Cameron Burns
Fists of Fury!'

Neil Neill
We cannae both be 'Fists'
I was 'Fists' first, *Fucker.*

Cameron
I need the 'fists'.

(*Bobby enters.*)

Neil Neill
Ye'll get the fists!
These fists you fucking future star!

(*And is about to punch out Cameron.*)

I am Neil Neill Fists of Steel and I *intend* to be a *star*

Bobby breaks up the ruck.

Bobby
Stars???

Youse lot???
Dream *on*!

Punishment push-ups!
For dirty fighting!!

(*All do punishment push-ups.*)

What makes a star?
What makes you earthbound blobs of shite intae a
glittering star in the boxing firmament???
Hard bloody graft!
It takes four bloody years before your light reaches us!
Fact!!!
Who made the stars?
Who made the universe?
Who???

All
God!

Bobby
Who's God?

Boys / Dina
You are!

Bobby
I'm *God*
Who Am I?

Boys / Dina
God!

Bobby
I'm *King Robert*
King Robert   The *Bruise*!
Who Am I?

Boys / Dina
King Robert   *The Bruise!!!*

Bobby

You obey *my* discipline
You follow all *my* rules
You practise *my* good behaviour
I teach you *my* moves
So you no come to harm if *I* can help it
That's what it's all aboot
Any *stars'll* be up there because *I've* made them
twinkle!!!

And they are all exhausted . . .

EIGHT
A BOXER'S STAFF, PART ONE

The washing machine rises again from the floor . . .
Carlotta, with clean tops for all . . .

Carlotta

Which soap powder would you recommend
For the removal of sweat?
and   blood   ???
oh aye *blood*
we all *love* the blood, don't we!
roll up roll up
come watch your boy
magically turn black and blue
see someone change his face frae 'handsome' tae 'Shrek'
watch his ears blossom intae cauliflowers . . .
'You're letting your son participate in a dangerous
sport, Missus???'
'How can you *live* with yourself???'
In my defence, your honour . . .
I've googled it extensively . . .
It's *amateur* boxing
That's really really low-level risk and . . .

apparently
He's learning
Tae defend himself
Tae learn skills
Tae learn self-control . . .   Please God
In mitigation
Your honour
Ladies and gentlemen o' the jury
What I have is . . .
A wain with more energy than the National Grid!
Cuddling him . . .
Is like holding a big lit firework . . .
You know it's going tae go off
You just never know when . . .
Or no   one of those big stripy tom cats that live wild
in sheds
He's up over your shoulder and doon yer back and off!
Before you can get hold of him . . .
Just like that skank-shagger of a bloody father . . .
At least noo I know where he is
At least noo I can hunt the wee disappearing daft
bastard doon . . .

Zanussi   Do you have a programme for 'Nose-Bleeds-
Heavy' . . .?

Didn't think so!!!

(*And she exits as . . .*)

NINE
DINA, DINA, NO ONE'S MEANER

Dina rises from the floor . . .

Dina
You can wipe that 'what the fuck's *she* daeing there?'

off your faces.

School said

'You're a *little* bit oot o' control, Dina dear, why *is* that?'

'Fuck off!'

They said 'Try tennis!

You clearly like *smashin* and *lobbin* stuff, Dina Massie!'

Fuck off.

They said 'A lot of the girls like to learn dance!'

If I want tae dance I'll go tae a fucking *club*

Fuck off!

They said 'What aboot *drama*!

I want you to improvise a scene with Carleen where you're trying to tell your mother you might be *pregnant . . .*'

Fuck   off!

Can't you fucking *see*

I'm wind I'm sleet I'm storm I'm black clouds

I'm the worst weather front you'll ever meet!

Don't fuckin come *near* me . . .

Don't fuckin think aboot it!

I'll pull your balls off and stuff them doon your gawpingaspin throat so you can have them for breakfast!!!

I'll *kill* you!

TEN
GOOD BOXING AND BAD BOXING

And they are all sparring . . .

Bobby

    Be subtle

    Don't hurt the air . . .

Dina

    Air's all I get tae hurt . . .

Bobby

Then why don't you
Go tae *women's* boxing . . .?

Dina

I don't want to do *women's* boxing, Bobby!
That's fucking 'boxercise' shite
I want to do *boxing*
I don't want you giving me your 'women's boxing's
Really getting more profile these days Olympic
coverage blah blah fucking blah you could go a long
way in women's boxing what do you think?' shite!

Bobby

It's *not* shite!
And I didn't say / boxercise

Dina

If it's *not* shite . . .
Then *you* train women's boxing . . .

(*She waits for his response.*
Nothing.)

(*Dripping sarcasm.*) After all   *that's* where the big
money is, right?!
That's where the sponsorship deals is, right?
That's where the global media coverage is, right?!

(*Waits again . . .*)

Aye, *right*!!!

Bobby

You'd get to *spar*

Dina

Aye, against *lassies*!
I'm same as *you*, Bobby . . .
I want to be the Main Event
No the Side Show!

Let me spar *here*
I want to do *boxing* boxing!

Bobby

Then stop *nagging*
And *do* fucking *boxing* boxing!
Ajay Chopra . . . stop *showboating*!!
You're *boxing*!

Ajay

Right.

Bobby

No *acting the bloody clown*!!!

Ajay

Right . . .
But . . . see . . . if I do this . . .
I invite him to come to me . . .
I piss him off . . .
He loses it . . .
I challenge him to take doon the clown . . .
I *appear* to be open to him . . . but . . .
Meanwhile . . . I get to watch him . . . see where *he's*
going to punch . . .
And effectively *counter* punch . . .
And he's doon
What do you think?

Bobby

Listen tae me
Listen tae me
Do what I *say*.
What I *say*.
Showboating
that's when your opponent
Is most dangerous tae you
When you're tired

That's when there's most *blood*, boy!
So you *mind* that!

Ajay

But . . .
Here's my point . . . Bobby . . .
It's also when *I'm* most dangerous to my opponent
Because I've made him underestimate me!
I *win*.

Bobby

But not in a good way.

Ajay

Good boxers are *liars*, Bobby
We promise one thing, deliver another.

Bobby

Good boxers *box*, Ajay.
We *box* well.
We box *clean*.
Will you remember that?

Ajay

I remember everything.

Bobby

You're an *elephant*, are you???

Ajay

I'm a *cobra*
I'm a *champion*

Bobby

You're a champion when *I* say you're a champion.
Who's God?

Ajay

You are, Bobby.

Bobby
Who do you *listen* to . . . ?

Ajay
You, King Bobby . . . I listen to *you*.

Bobby
On you go.

ELEVEN
AMATEUR TIME

Boxing arena.

Bobby
Okay   soon   ye'll be fighting other lads frae other clubs
Ye need tae know how that works . . .
Ainsley Binnie and Neil Neill will show us how *they* think it should go . . .
The rest of us is attentive crowd . . .

Cameron (*to Ajay*)
Crisp?

Ajay
No!

Cameron
Crisp?

Dina
No!

Cameron
Crisp, Bobby?

Bobby
What's *this*???

Cameron
Crisps

Bobby
Can't hear you

Cameron
Crisps

Bobby
Can't hear you . . . ?

Cameron
Junk, Bobby.

Bobby
Junk, twat.
Ajay . . . ?

Ajay
Food is   Fuel Energy Potential, Twat.

Bobby
Listen and Learn, Twat.

Dina
You Twatty Twat.

Bobby
You will be holding their little hands through all their
amateur fights . . .

(*Neil Neill enters in helmet and gumshield.*)

Neil Neill (*incomprehensible*)
Bobby . . . did you put me in the blue corner or the red
corner only I cannae remember . . . I was in the blue
corner in Lanark but I was in the red corner in
Kirkaldy . . .
I think it was the blue corner.
No wait a minute . . .

I think it was the *red* corner . . .
Bobby . . .

(*Ainsley enters in helmet and gumshield.*)

Ainsley (*also incomprehensible*)
Bobby . . . will you check this chin strap because the
other lads have been messing with my kit and I think
it's got loose and possibly dangerous . . .
And some monkey's put bubble gum in my boots again
and I think it was *either* Cameron Burns *or* Neil
bloody Neill . . .

Bobby
Idiot Boys   listen to me

Anything you want to say to anybody before a match
You have to say *before* you put your gumshields in . . .
Okay?

Neil Neill / Ainsley
Yes Bobby sorry Bobby didn't think Bobby

Bobby
Go to your corners, Twats.

(*Carlotta, almost Sam Spade like, enters furtively.*)

Carlotta (*to us*)
One night
I track him down
I follow the telltale trail of crisps
Through the broken glass . . .
Across the deserted wasteland
And into 'the mother ship'

(*And for the first time, she's watching live boxing . . .*)

Bobby
'And its Ainsley Binnie frae the Bobby Burgess Gym
fighting

Neil Neill also
Frae the Bobby Burgess gym!
What a Nurturer o' Young Talent this man is!'

Carlotta
I just want to burst out *greetin*!

Bobby
Ye have to train a lot of toads
Before ya find a boxing prince . . .

Carlotta
All these Beautiful Young Lads
Standing like   *Gladiators*

Bobby
Most amateur contests . . .
It's like watching a coupla *hares* in a field . . .
Raise your guard
Your jaw's connected to your legs!
Surprise! Not power!

Carlotta
And
I get it
I get why he loves it . . .
It gets into you . . .

(*And makes her shout . . .*)

Move your feet!

Duck!

It's as good as sex   but no so *complicated.*

Bobby
See how safe you are in there if you *think*?

Carlotta
And I see
Helmets on their daft wee heads

Big squashy gloves!
And . . . look! . . .
Nobody hits anybody!

They don't . . .

Bobby
Keep your balance at all times
Walking
Nice and relaxed nice and relaxed

Carlotta
And I see someone's *watching out* for them

Bobby
Nice and loose
Slip bang punch

Carlotta
And   I see
My stripy wee cat
Actually *listening* to someone telling him how to behave

Bobby
Slip to the inside
Slip to the outside

Carlotta
And I see   he's *safe* here

Bobby
Step inside now
Good!

Bobby
You want to be champions?
You want to be pros?

Carlotta
I can see them all get   *brighter*
There's   like   a smile in their   bodies . . .

Neil Neill

Magic!!!

Ainsley

When a nerve impulse reaches the spinal chord . . .
Endorphins are released
Which stop the nerve cells from releasing more pain
signals
It allows the body to feel a sense of power
And have control over itself
Fact.

Carlotta

'Endorphins'   *weird* word innit?
In my head
I get this *picture*
The *end* of the world
Far far away
And in   sparkling sea . . .
*Dolphins   en*dolphins
Mental . . . Right?

(*She makes to go.*
  She with her endolphins . . .)

Bobby

It needs to be relentless

Carlotta

See you boys!

(*They ignore her.*)

The Gladiators
Ignore her
She is after all   a mere female *mother*.

(*She exits.*)

Bobby

> It needs tae be relentless
> Ye need tae be *relentless*
> Because
> In the no sae *salubrious* parts o' different toons . . .
> No just Greenock! No just Arbroath Forgewood
> Wellmeadow Kirkintilloch
> No just Sleigh Drive Edinburgh
> There's gyms *everywhere*
> Where's lads are waiting tae punch *you*!

Cameron

> Things I give up for this.
> Shoplifting.
> Borrowing cars.
> Smoking. Tobacco *and* weed.
>
> *Girlfriends.*
> I still dae *Shagging* . . .
> But only on Friday and Saturday.
> I jest cannae dae the *Commitment* Thing wi lassies.
> What else . . .???
> Crisps
> Spare time.
> Spare time . . .
> Whit's *that*?

Bobby

> Just make a few more sacrifices
> Just give more time
> Because in the East End of London
> In the Bloody East End of *Europe* Ukraine Latvia
> Georgia

Fucking 'All Star Gym, Hackensack, New Jersey'
Fucking 'Golden Child Boxing Gym, Mandalingong
City'
Lads are getting fitter faster tae fucking fight *you*
Luckily for *you*
In the luxurious surroundings
of a wee made-over scout hut in Glamorous Glasgow
something good's happening.
His lads are growing up growing out
but
they're staying *with* him
training furiously *with* him   and
Bobby Burgess . . . formerly a cup-half-empty-man . . .
Starts believing in fairy tales
Starts believing in   'He lives happily ever after'
that
There might just be a cloud with a silver lining for him
There might be just a wee pot of gold at the end of this
particular rainbow . . .
Because
Slowly   but surely
In a world formerly full of *frogs* . . .
Some *princes* start tae emerge . . .
As
A lot of them
As they get older . . .
Just get *better*

(*And they perform an impressive display of
improvement and growing up.*)

THIRTEEN
FOUR LIGHT YEARS LATER

Bobby with training pads . . .

Bobby
I can see for myself   just a wee bit more money
I can feel   the possibility of *success* . . .
Because I hit my lucky streak
Two nights turn to three into four into five
Things are starting to cook
The ingredients the recipes working
Talent's beginning to twinkle
Among the fighting frogs
I'm finding my princes . . . and . . .
Princes are like buses . . . you wait ages for one . . .
Then three or four come along all at once!

This is my hot prospect –

Ajay 'The Cobra' Chopra
I'm pinning my hopes on this one
If I can just keep him *here*
Under *control*!
Born to it
Watch . . .
Speed   Intelligence . . . Talent
This one –
'Professor' Ainsley Binnie
Steady hardworking but . . . no sure . . .
Too much 'booksblogswebsitefact!' . . .
This one –
Neil Neill
Fists of Steel
Maniac but on a good day *magic* . . .
You're just never sure what day that's gonnae *be* . . .
Look at this one, Dina Massie The Battling Lassie . . .

If she were a boy . . .
I could take her to the top of the mountain
Make her the brightest star in the sky
We'd both own big huge houses
Our own Mercedes . . .

Dina
BMWs.

Bobby
If she'd only contemplate the world of *women's* boxing
She could . . .

Dina
Drive a Robin Reliant!
Live in a fucking *shed*!
Put your money where your mouth is, Bobby,
Take me *on*
You do a Clint Eastwood
Train me for pro women's stuff . . .
Help me become a *real* Million Dollar Baby
But without the shite ending!

Bobby
Stop the nagging
Do the boxing!

Dina
We could be a team!
You and me!
Think about it!

Bobby
Alright! Jesus!

This one –
Cameron Burns
Great *instinctive* boxer brilliant stamina   joined me
late . . . still a bit behind still a bit *attitude* . . .
Nae Einstein . . .

Looks like a wee white mouse
But with the heart of a lion . . .
Seems like   a wee cheap ukulele
Plays like a Fender Stratocruiser . . .
Go on, son
Ajay Chopra!!!
I don't know what you're doing but you're no doing
what I told you!

Ajay

I'm trying something new.

Bobby

You're *trying* my patience!!!

And *I* just want you to do as you're told, you arrogant
bloody . . .!

Massey
Show me your jab.
Rubbish
Show me your hook
Rubbish
I don't know why you bother.

Dina

Aye you do.

'This is Sandy
He is your new stepdaddy
Say hello to Uncle Sandy
Well Dina
You're a pretty wee girl come and sit on Uncle Sandy's
knee . . .'

Bobby

Your mother's dafter than ever

Dina

You should have married her

Bobby

No, I should just have adopted *you*.
You want *me* to come sort Uncle Sandy oot?

Dina

No. I'm a Big Girl.
I'll sort him oot *myself*.

Bobby

Boxing's no aboot *revenge*

Dina

It *is* from where I'm standing!
Don't be a dinosaur, Bobby . . .
Work with me!
Make it aboot BMWs!

Bobby

Ainsley Binney, what you looking at???

Ainsley

Nothing

Bobby

Look somewhere else

Ainsley

Okay

Bobby

Put your eyes back in your head
And
Sort your hands out, you look like a fuckin boxing kangaroo!
Let's go let's go let's see you kill it
Cameron Burns
It's your shoulder carries your guard.
Watch *this maniac*

Just like I telled ye . . . *Good!*

(They practise their weaknesses . . .)

Dina

You are the Main Event!
You are Prime Time!

Ainsley

You are *not* a boxing kangaroo!

You are *not* a boxing kangaroo!

You are *not* a boxing kangaroo!

Neil Neill

You are *not* a maniac!

You have Fists of Steel!

Cameron

It's like a fucking *marathon*
You started back of the fucking field
You didn't even *hear* the fucking starting pistol
So you're fucking running running running
Just to fucking catch up on the leaders!!
Come *on*, Cameron!
Catch *up*!
Draw *level*!
Fucking *sail past them*!!!

FOURTEEN
THREE FAVOURITE SONS

Bobby

And the day arrives . . .
When half-cup-full Bobby Burgess
Decides to turn his frogs
Intae princes . . .

Ajay Chopra
Cameron Burns

48

Neil Neill . . .
I want you to think about turning pro

Neil Neill
YESSSSS!!!

Cameron
You caught them *up*!
Fucking *ace*!!!

Dina
Well . . .
Thanks, Clint!

Bobby
Massie!

Dina
I'll be doing ma *boxercise* over in the corner, okay . . .

(*Very girly mime . . .*)

Bobby
Dina . . .
I just don't want *you* hurt.

Dina
This hurts more.
Hypocrite!
Dinosaur!
Fuck off!

Ajay
I have already been thinking / this is a good plan.

Bobby
I'm prepared to train you myself
Manage all your business and paperwork
But   it's *three* of you
It's a fuck of a lot of work from *me*
So I want two hundred per cent commitment from all
of *youse* . . .

Cameron / Ajay / Neil
Aye alright

Bobby
I want you to talk to your parents

Cameron
Aye   *Alright!!!*

Neil Neill
Is it alright if it's my Care Coordinator, Bobby?

Bobby
Care Coordinator/Parents/Parole Officer whatever . . .
Ainsley Binney, what you looking at???

Ainsley
Nothing

Bobby
Look somewhere else

Ainsley
Okay

Bobby
See if I can hook you up with a promoter, sort oot
some money

Ajay
My uncle the property investor is interested in –

Bobby
Okay

Ajay
– discussing funding with you

Bobby
Early days yet . . . we want tae start slow and care/ful
okay?

Ajay

He has a conglomerate of businessmen –

Bobby

Okay . . .

Ajay

– who have seed money –

Bobby

Early days . . .

Ajay

– that they're looking tae ring/fence

Bobby

'Early days'
Early days! Jesus!!!

FIFTEEN
WHAT'S IN THE FRIDGE

A fridge arrives . . .
Carlotta puts her hot head in it . . .

Carlotta

I'm pretending I'm defrosting my fridge
I'm pretending I'm discovering what's hidden in the
frozen wastes of the freezer compartment . . .
It's snow white snow as far as the eye can see
and an iceberg the size of *Aberdeen*   he wants tae go
professional!

Cool it!
Chillax!

Noooooooooooooooooooooo!
Just bear with me a moment . . .
Until I've processed this

Wrapped it in *clingfilm*
Freezed it and put it in here till its *sell-by date*
like every other one of my *Terrors*!!!
Amateur . . .
He was *safe* . . .
He had a huge daft helmet on his soft head!
Professional . . .
That's aboot folk with the money saying
We've *paid* for this . . .
What we want is *blood*
What we want is *damage*
That's what we're paying tae see!

It'll be alright
It may never happen.
Things come to nothing.
Dreams die.
Cool it!

SIXTEEN
OUT INTO THE COLD COLD SNOW

Sparring practice. Ajay is winding Neil Neill up . . .

Neil Neill
Fuck Off!!

Bobby
Oh for *fuck's sake*!!!

Showboating!

Again!!!

Again with the *Humiliating*!

What did I tell you?

Ajay
You told me to do as you tell me.

Bobby

So why didn't you *do* as I tell you?

Jesus *Christ*!!!

Ajay

Because   I don't always think you know better than me

Bobby

Don't you?

Ajay

Because   I have applied myself rigorously to the study
of my style
Which is significantly *different* from everybody else's
and . . .
Bloody *effective*.

Bobby

You think . . .???

Ajay

Yes.
And
And
Because   we should be able to discuss things . . . and
agree on strategies . . .
If I'm going pro we need to agree on a thought-through
style of attack . . .

Bobby

Get your kit.

Ajay

What?

Bobby

Get your kit. And go.
Here . . . your subs back. Go spend it at another gym.
I need boxers who *know* who / knows best.

Ajay

I was just
Wait
No
This is banal.   *Bobby!!!*

Bobby

It's finished.
Over.

Ajay

I'm the best boxer here
I have the best brain
I have the best style
I'm turning pro
You want me to turn pro
You're my trainer . . .
Bobby!   This is *banal.* Can't we . . .

Bobby

Ajay!!!
Try *listen* for once!
Listening is how you *Learn.*
Hard Facts
I'm gonnae be Cameron Burns' trainer.
I'm gonna be Neil Neill's trainer
I might even God help us be Ainsley Binnie's trainer

Ainsley

Yesss!
Thanks, Bobby!

Bobby

No you.

Dina

Thanks, Bobby

54

Ajay

Can't we discuss this . . . ?
Are we not going to discuss this???

Bobby

Discussing is exactly what this is aboot!
I'm running a *boxing* gym, no *A Question ae Sport*!
Discipline's aboot *obedience*

Ajay

Not *blind* obedience, shouldn't a boxer *think*???

Bobby

He should think aboot boxing
Not the *humiliation* of his opponent.

Ajay

It helps tae *win*.
It's what the crowd *likes*.

Bobby

Get your kit.
Get out my gym.
Find yourself somewhere that *likes* you tae win like
that.

Ajay

Thank you, Bobby.
I wish you every success.
I wish everyone here every success.

Bobby

Ainsley Binnie.

Ainsley

Yes, Bobby!

Bobby

Did you hear all that?

Ainsley

No, Bobby.

Bobby

Not absolutely definitely *you* yet, understand . . . ?

Ainsley

Yes, Bobby.

Bobby

Ainsley Binnie!
Neil Neill! Stairs! Now!
Cameron Burns!
Dina Massie!
You two are finished now.
See the lassie safe home okay?

Cameron

I'm no sure the Lassie will *let* me see her safe home . . .

Dina

'The Lassie' can see herself safe home!

Bobby

Just do what you're told – both of you!

You can't have a *democracy*
Your reign's got to be *absolute*!
Good decision
Good decision!
Fuck!!!

SEVENTEEN
'WE HAVE NOTHING BUT TIME'

Cameron and Dina among stars . . .

Cameron

What's the point?

Dina

What's what point?

Cameron

The point of *you*.

Dina

What?

Cameron

What's the point of *you* boxing?

Dina

What's the point of *you* boxing?

Cameron

I'm training tae a peak of superb physical fitness

Dina

I'm training tae a peak of superb physical fitness

Cameron

And . . .

Dina

And . . .?

Cameron

I'm going tae be a fuckin champion and fuckin famous
with a fistful of fuckin money

Dina

I'm going tae be fuckin toned and gorgeous and take
nae shit frae any fuckin wannabe champion scrawny

And a fuckin champion

And fucking famous

With a fuckin enormous fistful o' fuckin money.

Cameron

So what's your name in lights again?

Dina
You *know* what my name in lights is!

Cameron
Oh aye.   Tits.

Dina
Tits o' *Terror.*

Cameron
Nice name.
O' Terror.

Is that Irish?

You want tae go for a drink?

Dina
A drink?

Cameron
Then you'll be able to say
'I knew him before he was famous'
'I knew him before he had fistfuls of fuckin money.'

Dina
Just a *drink* . . .?

(*Cameron takes out his money. They both look at it.*)

Just a small drink

(*Dina gets out her money . . .*)

With peanuts.

Cameron
'Protein'

It's a *date* then, 'Tits'?

Dina
It's a date, 'Fistfuls of Fucking Money'.

EIGHTEEN

THESE CRUELLY IGNORED BUT
MOST RESILIENT OF THE BURGESS STABLE

Dina putting on her gloves as . . .

Ainsley
Alright   Dina?

Dina
Can't see you

Ainsley
If you need any help back-up feedback type thing

Dina
Can't hear you

Ainsley
Occupied. Right?
Focused. Right?
I get it.
Respect.

Bobby
Ainsley Binnie.

Ainsley
Yes, Bobby?

Bobby
Okay.
Thing is . . .
I'm a bit *pressed* with Cameron and Neil and their
schedules and setting up matches and paperwork and
legwork and shite . . .

Ainsley
Yes, Bobby

Bobby

I have tae *prioritise*
So I'm *devolving* you tae Auld Alec and Whammo for
training

Ainsley

Oh. But . . . Couldn't . . . It's just . . .
Auld Alec and Whammo . . . ?

Bobby

They'll be able tae give you more time than I can . . .

Ainsley

But . . .
Okay Yes Bobby Got it
Understand
Completely

Bobby

Good lad.

(*Dina on punchbags, working furiously.
Neil Neill takes over her bag.*)

Dina

What the fuck?

Neil Neill

Precedence thing.
Pro stuff.
Bobby says.

Dina moves to the next punchbag.
(*Cameron enters.*)

Cameron

Alright?

Dina

Alright.

Cameron

Bobby says I have tae put three minutes in on this . . .
Pro stuff.
Preference thing.

Dina

Alright

(*She holds the bag for him . . .
   He punches.*)

Nice.

You wanta go for a *small drink* later?

Cameron

I'm no drinking.

Dina

You wanta go for *a bag of dry-roasted peanuts* later?

Cameron

I'm no eating shite.

Dina

Just a nice little walk . . . ?

Cameron

I've got tae concentrate
No distractions if I want to be a pro.
Bobby says.

(*Dina walks away.*)

Ainsley

This cruelly ignored but still unbeaten supermiddleweight
This most resilient of the Burgess stable
Learns the hardest lesson of his career . . .
Patience   that virtue of the very best
He's gonna get *Zen*
He's quite spiritual this imperious quietly impressive
contender . . .

Pushed to the limits of his considerable ability
Regarded as the underdog
His time will come

(*He sees Dina punching . . .*)

No . . . Dina

Sweetheart   You need to . . .

(*Dina punches Ainsley. He falls to the ground.*)

Dina
Jesus fuckin Christ just some space just some fuckin
space!!!
Not all!
Not half!
Just some!!!

Ainsley
I don't know what you're talking / aboot . . .
I was just trying to help.

Dina
No! You Don't!
Fact!

Ainsley
That was just   lucky

Dina
That was *boxing*!
D'you   even *know* how good I am????
D'you even know how much I like no fuckin *love*
The sweat the hittin the punching the –
How much I want tae hit be hit compete get blooded up
feel someone's nose bones go crunch under my hand
Feel the fuckin breath leave somebody's fuckin
stomach????
Punch me back!

Ainsley

No

Dina

Punch me back, you fuckin coward.

Ainsley

No.

Dina

So you punch me in the breast?
So you put me on the floor?
I'll *kill* you!!!
Fuckin punch me!!!

Ainsley

No
I don't *want* to!!!
Sorry, Dina.

Dina

Oh   *fuck!!*

(*She realises where she is heading . . .*)

No
I'm sorry
Boxing's about skill and discipline.

(*She collects her stuff.*)

It's not about *rage*.
Its too dangerous.
I shouldnae be here
I'm not a boxer
I'm a fucking *killer*
And
Ainsley . . .

It *was* just lucky.
Sorry.

(*She exits.*)

NINETEEN
BREATH

Neil Neill and Cameron running and sweating . . .

Neil Neill
Fucking Bobby!

Cameron
That *bastard*!

Neil Neill
He's *killing* us!

Cameron
Right
The *bastard*!
D'you see Ajay on the telly last night?

Neil Neill
Pure *brilliant*!
Magic!

Cameron
Could *you* take him?

Neil Neill
Could I????
That showboating fucker????
Put me in a ring with him, Bobby Fucking Burgess!!!
Could You???

Cameron
Could I???
Get me the fucking contest, Bobby!!!
I'll knock his fucking head off his fucking shoulders
I'll punch his fucking lights out
I'll put him doon.

(Bobby enters as . . .)

He'll never get up
If Bobby would just pull your fucking finger out
And promote the fuck oot of me
And put me up against him
Bobby fucking Burgess . . .

(*Notices Bobby.*)

Both

Alright, Bobby!

Mr Burgess.

TWENTY
ARRESTED PUNCHES

Bobby, with practice gloves.

Bobby

Where we're at at this particular moment in time is as
follows . . . I'm talking tae Frank Warren, Frank
Warren's talking tae Chopra's fuckin uncles, and
entourage and shite so we basically got a match wi the
Asian Super-Cobra once we're all agreed on the nuts
and fucking bolts . . .
But only *one* o' you fists can be *first* . . .
The decision is *mine*
Its all still tae play for.

Okay, contestants
The Time has come
I have a place for just one contender.
Who is it gonna be?
Let's see what's in those fists
Let's see what's in those heads
Let's see you think for yourselves.

(*And they box, with arrested punches.*)

Cameron
Your brain is in *ma* head
Your expertise is in *ma* hands
Your dreams are in *here*.

Neil Neill
Twenty-seven bones to *one* bone
Get me Ajay, Bobby

Cameron
Let me get Ajay for you, Bobby

Cameron
Ya bastard

Neil Neill
Ya bastard . . .

Bobby
Good that, Neil Neill.
Good contender

Neil Neill –
Magic

Bobby –
Sorry, son
Next time maybe . . .
Keep on keeping on . . .

(*Bobby leaves stage with Neil Neill.*)

Cameron
Oh *fuck*!
Look at this *vest*!

Twenty-five fucking *quid*!
Cameron's making shite money
Cameron's nae social life

Cameron's scrabbling around for a match
But Cameron's a *pro* boxer
He's Somebody Tae *Watch*!!!

But . . .
And where's he gonna get the suede lockdoon hi-top
boots at 135 quid, pro-fight gloves at £150 the pair
new punch mitts focus mitts handwraps bag gloves he
needs he's fucking haemorrhaging money . . .????
Fuck!
Let me have it!
It's not much to ask!
Then
I start tae earn.
No more scratching around for coins
Subbing off your parents!
Soon you're saying . . .
'Here Mum, treat yourself'
'Dad . . . Sheila . . . buy yourself a *car*
The *Audi Megane* . . .?   No problem!
Mum?   D'you like this house?
Here. Keys!
Whose?
Mine! I bought it with my advertising???
For you.
It's yours.'
Who do I run into?
'Hey, Tits!
Hey   Dina
Yes . . .
That *was* me on the telly, yes . . .
Yes . . . noo . . . with lassies . . . It *is* like Bees round
this Honeypot oh yes . . .
Dina, Dina, Dina I warned you tae
Date early tae avoid disappointment
Dina?
We could go out *now*?
Got the money *now*!
Dina?'

(*But she's nowhere . . .*)

Ajay, dressed like a superstar . . .

Ajay

    Every day's mad . . . be the figurehead on this project
    Be the name on that project . . .
    I glaze over.
    It's like there's two mes.
    I'm not just Ajay Chopra.
    I'm Ajay Chopra, Pro Boxer   Contender
    Role model   Icon.
    Asian Star.
    The Spitting Cobra!
    Are ye catching all this
    King Bobby?
    God Bobby???
    Ruler of your tiny wee universe?
    Are ye reading about me Bobby, in your pathetic wee
    local paper?
    Are ye watching me on your wee rented telly in your
    sad little council hoose?
    Try *listen* for once, Bobby.
    'Listening is how you *Learn*.'

    Short Punjabi history lesson, Bobby fucking Burgess!

    My rhythms are hundreds of years old
    My roots are long and strong and deep
    It's what makes me a *Winner*
    This is the champion!   Here!   *This!*
    Fuck you, Bobby Burgess . . .
    Fuck you, Neil Neill
    Fists of Steel?
    Balloons for Brains!
    Listen to all the people that *like* me tae win like *this*!

Don't ever turn ye back on a *cobra*, Bobby
It'll just store up its poison until it can *strike*!
Don't get up
Don't.

TWENTY-TWO
BOXING IS SAFER THAN CROSSING A ROAD

*Ainsley, optimistic, in a darkened gym . . . talking to a
non-existent Dina . . .*

Ainsley
Hi Dina! Yes! Thanks.
Since I sought out alternative medicine
Touch wood never been ill.
My immune system is immaculate.
Fact.
Two litres of water and 100 mg of Vitamin C every
four hours
Vit C is a natural virus fighter so fresh OJ or a peeled
orange . . . magic

I don't think . . . if you tried *now* . . . you'd be able to
land one on me again!
That was funny wasn't it!
That was hilarious!
So Dina . . .
You want to hear something else funny?
Something really hilarious . . . ?
Okay . . . Boxing
If you play by *the rules* . . .
It's statistically safer than crossing a road! Fact!

(*He becomes aware of Neil Neill, prowling the
perimeter, a lot drunk . . .*)

It's all about *supervision* . . .

Structure . . .
Safety   that's why they
Check you immediately before the fight
Eyes Mouth Ears Back It's a Game It's a Sport
It's mostly about
Surprise
Surprise
Not power!
Lungs Heart
The game's simple . . .
Administer a shock to the nervous system
Overload his brain . . .
So it crashes
Hands Forearms XBox but with a real body
Right?
The last death in amateur boxing right here in
Scotland
Was *1952*!
Fact.
Accidents in boxing even professional boxing
Are rarer than you might think and
Okay   the BMA *are* totally against boxing
But   honestly . . .
The studies are inconclusive . . .
Boxing isn't even the most dangerous sport!
Fact!

Neil Neill
Good tae know!

Ainsley
Try horseriding!

Neil Neill
Giddee *up*!

Ainsley
They keep five beds at the hospital

Every Saturday night
For *Rugby*
Fact.

Neil Neill
Up and under!

Ainsley
Climbing Ben Nevis is more dangerous

Neil Neill
Ah, right

Ainsley
Mostly   injury-wise   you're lucky
Fact.

(*Neil Neill, dangerous, mauls Ainsley . . .
     Ainsley lets him.*)

Neil Neill
Okay . . .
Here's a *fact* . . .
Boxing never hurts *me* . . .
I'm no a statistic o' boxing
I'm crossing Renfield Street one Saturday night oot . . .
Fucking *taxi* full of lassies on a *hen* night I don't see it
comin
Bang!!!
And the taxi driver gets out and I can smell it on his
breath, he says
'Are ye alright, pal . . .?
Give us yer hand . . .
Och what's happened tae yer hand???

And look at his leg his leg his leg's oh *fucked* . . .'
I'm a statistic o' drink driving!
Life fucks me
No boxing.

Nae bother . . . plenty of boxers out there . . .
Twenty-seven bones smashed to fuck
Turns me intae a *spectator*
Total fucking spectator!!!
I was this close.
Look . . .

(*Gets out . . . reads . . .*)

A ringside seat ticket tae the championship contest
between Ajay Chopra and late substitution Cameron
'Fists ae Shite' Burns!!
Now   *that's* funny!!!

That's fucking *hilarious*!

TWENTY-THREE
TWELVE THREE-MINUTE ROUNDS

Bobby is wrapping Cameron's hands . . .
Carlotta, dressed to kill, with hand cream . . .

Carlotta
It's okay
It's alright
It's all good.

(*She opens the hand cream.*)

Bobby
Alright, son?

Cameron
Alright, Bobby.

Carlotta
Your honour
In mitigation of my crime in sending my only son –

(*Starts applying it . . .*)

– intae the bloody mean money-grabbing manipulative
face-mashing body-smashing world
Of professional boxing . . .
I would argue . . .
He's fucking *brilliant* at it!

Bobby
All the best, son

Cameron
Thank you.   Mr Burgess.

Carlotta
It makes him *special* tae the *world*!
It shortens the odds on him getting somewhere in life.
There's an ootside chance ma son's gonnae *count*!

Bobby
Ready?

(*Cameron puts up his hands. They are things of
beauty.*)

Cameron
Aye   alright

Carlotta (*her hands are things of beauty*)
These are *my* precision instruments
I'll be doing a lot o' clapping. Oh yes.
A *lot* of clapping!

(*Three Referees dance their dance.
    At the end, one of them becomes Dina, dressed as a
Ring Girl . . .*)

Dina
You can wipe that 'what the fuck's *she* daeing there?'
off your faces.
You'll watch me go twelve rounds now
I'm wind I'm sleet I'm storm I'm black clouds
I'm 'Get 'em oot fe the lads' . . . I'm 'Camel Toe!' I'm

'A'd Gie Her One!'
I'm the worst weather front you'll ever meet!
Don't fuckin come *near* me . . .
Don't fuckin think aboot it!
I'll pull your balls off and stuff them doon your
gawpingaspin throat so you can have them for
breakfast!!!
I'll *kill* you!
Different ways of being a 'Fucking Killer', right
This is what training and discipline does for you . . .
Plus a little bit of judicious silicon . . .

(*Big fight . . . a dance of fighting, corners, rounds,
referees, spectators, mothers and contenders . . .
Which ends . . .*)

TWENTY-FOUR
BEAUTIFUL BURNOUT!

*Cameron has received a blow to his head . . .
All alone . . .*

Cameron
Stars

I was *going* somewhere . . . ?

Fuuuuuuuuuuuuuuuuuuuuuuuuuuuck   Stars!
Red planet Mars
Ma's
Look Ma, top of the world

Jupiter
Earth
Uranus   ha ha
Saturn Mars bars
Jupiter

74

Earth
Earth
Earth
Earth

(*Something breaks in his brain.*)

. . .
. . .
. . .
. . .
. . .
. . .
What the . . .?

(*He sees something he has never seen before from somewhere he has never been . . .*)

Oh fu—
Oh well . . .

(*But he now sees only . . .*)

Joooo
Yur
Saaaaa
Mmmm   mmmmm
Ur
Ur
Ur

TWENTY-FIVE
REFEREE DANCE

Steve George, in the ring but with remote, looks at footage of one particular moment from the fight . . .

Steve
   Watch like an eagle

Protect the boxer
Without fear or favour.

'Referee Steve George's questionable refereeing in the
twelfth round'
100,000 hits
Fuckin YouTube!!!
Gotta *love* modern technology

Let's see that *again*, again, Boxing Aficionados . . .

(*And presses 'replay' . . .*)

TWENTY-SIX
ONE PUNCH CAN GO ROUND THE WORLD:
FACT

Carlotta dresses Cameron as . . .
    Others, in civvies . . .

Ainsley
    There's this term 'Black Lights'
    In the Science World . . .
    It's the black portion of the electromagnetic spectrum
    Which is the domain of X-rays and radio waves.

Bobby
    Okay
    Ah might have made a wrong call   a few wrong calls
    Maybe I should have thrown in the towel

    But
    I didnae
    Hey
    Even *God* makes mistakes.

Ainsley
    It's also a term in boxing . . .
    Some boxers report seeing 'black lights'

76

Just before oblivion
They *see* and become *surrounded* by
This shimmering   glowing aura of darkness

Bobby
I visit Cameron
Once a month
On a Sunday
That's my only day off

Ainsley
This shimmering darkness
Is known medically as 'visual scotoma'
The afflicted brain is experiencing the paradox
Of being *conscious* of its *unconsciousness*

Dina
Well
he got what he wanted
He got tae fight with the whole world watching
He went twelve rounds
He defended himself tae the last
And
He *is* famous in a way.

Ajay
I won
I'm unconquerable
I remember *everything*

Breathe in

Breathe in . . .

Bobby
Don't believe in fairy tales
You have tae move on
You get one life
Time doesnae stand still
I make a call

I take over the training o' this likely lad frae Greenock.
. .
His brains are in his hands
He doesnae try tae hurt the air
And
He's *lucky*.

Ainsley

The *Reason* for this black lights phenomenon
When the higher cognitive centres of the brain shut
down
The lower areas
The *limbic* system
Kick in to preserve a primitive sense of awareness
Our human system sort of *organises* itself to *defend*
itself . . .
It's brilliant
It's *made* to fight
It *loves* fighting   the human body
Fact.

Neil Neill

What spectators do
Is
Watch
I take my *Rocky* box set round tae Cameron
We watch it all the time
That
And
The Champ
Except
The Champ's a bit *sad* for us . . .
We both greet like wee lassies . . .

(*All exit, leaving* . . .)

TWENTY-SEVEN
BLACK LIGHTS

Carlotta with Cameron . . .

Carlotta
The good news is
I get my wee boy back
I get my baby
My Cameron
I get him every minute of every hour of every day of
every week

Of every year but I get him back . . .

My stripy wee cat.

You're supposed to see stars
I hope you do
I hope you don't just see dark
I hope you see sky
Blue sky   sun
Or
The night sky
Wi shooting stars.

What you got in your head, my darlin?

What can you see, son?

(*The inside of his happy head as . . .*

End of Play.)